★ ★

WAR HEROES OF AMERICA

Robert E. Lee

THE SOUTH'S GREAT GENERAL

MATTHEW G. GRANT

Illustrated by John Keely

GALLERY OF GREAT AMERICANS SERIES

★ ★

Robert E. Lee

THE SOUTH'S GREAT GENERAL

Library of Congress Number: 73-18078   ISBN: 0-87191-302-X

Published by Creative Education, Mankato, Minnesota 56001
Distributed by Childrens Press, 1224 West Van Buren Street, Chicago, Illinois 60607

Library of Congress Cataloging in Publication Data
Grant, Matthew G
  Robert E. Lee; the South's great general.
  (His Gallery of great Americans series. War heroes of America)
  SUMMARY: An easy-to-read biography of the leader of the Confederate forces in the Civil War.
  1. Lee, Robert Edward, 1807-1870 — Juvenile literature. (1. Lee, Robert Edward, 1807-1870.
2. Generals. 3. United States — History — Civil War) I. Keely, John, illus. II. Title.
E467.1.L4G58   973.7'3'0924 (B) (92)   73-18078
ISBN 0-87191-302-X

CONTENTS

IMPORTANT BATTLES OF
ROBERT E. LEE

CADET FROM VIRGINIA

"Light Horse Harry" Lee had fought beside George Washington during the Revolution. His son, Robert, loved to hear him talk about those exciting days, when men of Virginia battled for freedom.

Brave Harry Lee was not a success in peacetime. He lost all his money. The family had to leave Stratford, the beautiful home where Robert had been born in 1807. They moved to Alexandria, Virginia.

In 1812, there was a riot and Harry Lee was hurt. He never really recovered. In 1818, he died, leaving Mrs. Ann Lee with five children to bring up. Robert was the fourth.

Young Robert was a serious-minded boy who loved to read. He also liked to ride and hunt. He decided that he would like to become a soldier, like his father. With the help of relatives who were important in government, Robert E. Lee was named a cadet at the U.S. Military Academy. He began his studies at West Point in 1825, when he was 18 years old.

He worked hard to become top man in his class.

The life of a West Point cadet was very hard. But Robert E. Lee seemed to thrive in spite of poor food, uncomfortable quarters, and endless difficult studies. He decided he wanted to become an army engineer. In his senior year, he was Number 2 in class standing and top man in drill. He was appointed cadet adjutant, a great honor, because of his leadership abilities. His kindness and natural good humor won him many friends.

He graduated in triumph and was commissioned a Second Lieutenant in the Corps of Engineers. After working on a fort in Georgia, he was transferred back to his home state of Virginia. He was able to spend time with his old friends and relations—especially his distant cousins of the Custis family, who were very rich. Robert fell in love with Mary Anne Custis. They were married in 1831.

WAR IN MEXICO

The next years were quiet. Lee was an excellent engineer and he had many different assignments. On one, he helped build dikes to prevent sand from choking the port at St. Louis, Missouri.

The United States went to war with Mexico in 1846. Captain Lee helped place the big guns that broke the walls of Veracruz, a Mexican port. American troops invaded Mexico at Veracruz and marched toward the capital, Mexico City, fighting as they went.

Lee helped scout the route through very difficult mountain country. He built bridges and roads. He dodged enemy troops and carried messages through the thick of battle.

American military leaders gave Lee high praise when the war ended in 1848. He was allowed to return home to his wife, who was living with her parents at the Custis mansion,

Arlington. It was here that the seven Lee children would grow up, while their father's army duties took him around the country. During the next ten years, Lee built a fort in Baltimore, served as Superintendent of West Point, and hunted Indians in Texas.

GENERAL IN GRAY

In 1859, he was sent with a force of marines to Harper's Ferry. He captured a man named John Brown, who had been inciting slaves to rebel. Brown was hanged. But his abolitionist ideas lived on.

Robert E. Lee saw his nation divided by the issue of slavery. He himself had freed his slaves, and the talk about seceding from the Union horrified him. But as matters drew to

a climax he knew he would have to choose

between his loyalty to Virginia and his loyalty

to the United States.

President Lincoln was prepared to offer

Lee command of an army that would subdue

the South.

But then Virginia seceded from the Union

in 1861. The very next day, Robert E. Lee

resigned his commission in the U.S. Army.

Almost overnight, Lee was appointed a major general in the Confederate Army. He helped advise President Jefferson Davis on military matters, especially the defense of the Confederate capital, Richmond, Virginia.

In 1862, 100,000 Union soldiers marched on the city.

Confederate General Johnston, who had been leading the Army of Northern Virginia, was wounded. The defense of Richmond was put into the hands of Robert E. Lee.

Even though he had fewer men, Lee used them well. For seven days he attacked the Union Army, scattering them and forcing them to draw back from the city. Lee's principal general in this fight was Thomas ''Stonewall'' Jackson. Working as a team, they drove the federal troops out of Virginia.

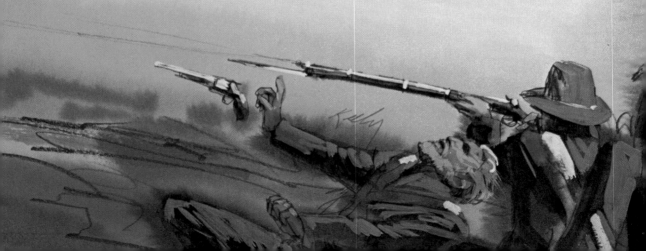

In his gray uniform, seated on his gray horse, Traveller, Lee led his men toward Washington. But by chance, his battle orders came into the hands of Union soldiers. His forces were trapped at Antietam Creek. Both armies fought valiantly, the North outnumbering the South by two to one. The Battle of

Antietam was a standoff that neither side could win. When it ended, Lee took his army back into Virginia.

Lincoln sent a new general, Ambrose Burnside, against Richmond the next winter. Lee defeated him at Fredericksburg, against great odds.

Lincoln sent General Joe Hooker after Lee the next spring. The rebel army—now ragged and hungry—had their most brilliant victory at the Battle of Chancellorsville, humiliating Hooker. But the South paid dearly. Stonewall Jackson was killed and Lee lost his best general.

THE ROAD TO APPOMATTOX

That summer of 1863 was the high point of the Civil War for the gray-clad Confederate forces. From then on, it was a long slide to disaster. Lee was badly defeated at Gettysburg. If only Stonewall Jackson had been alive!

Lincoln appointed General Ulysses S. Grant commander-in-chief. At last Lee was faced by a man whose military genius was equal to his own. The two armies met in spring, 1864, and fought the bloody Wilderness Campaign. Lee protected Richmond—but his losses were terrible. Furthermore, Grant did not withdraw as the other generals had done. His men laid waste the countryside. Other Union armies were marching through southern states. Lee knew the end was near.

In spring, 1865, Lee's men were starving and almost without supplies. Grant's soldiers had been reinforced. Faced by an army

three times the size of his own, Lee had
to retreat, leaving Richmond to be taken
by Grant.

Lee's army was surrounded near Appo-
mattox Court House. On April 9, 1865, Robert
E. Lee surrendered. He told his weeping men
to go to their homes.

The terrible Civil War was over.

The bravery and noble character of Robert E. Lee were respected by people of the South and North alike. He retired to private life and became the president of Washington College in Virginia. He helped to build it up into a prosperous university.

On October 12, 1870, Lee died. He was buried in a chapel on the university campus. After his death, the school was re-named Washington and Lee University.